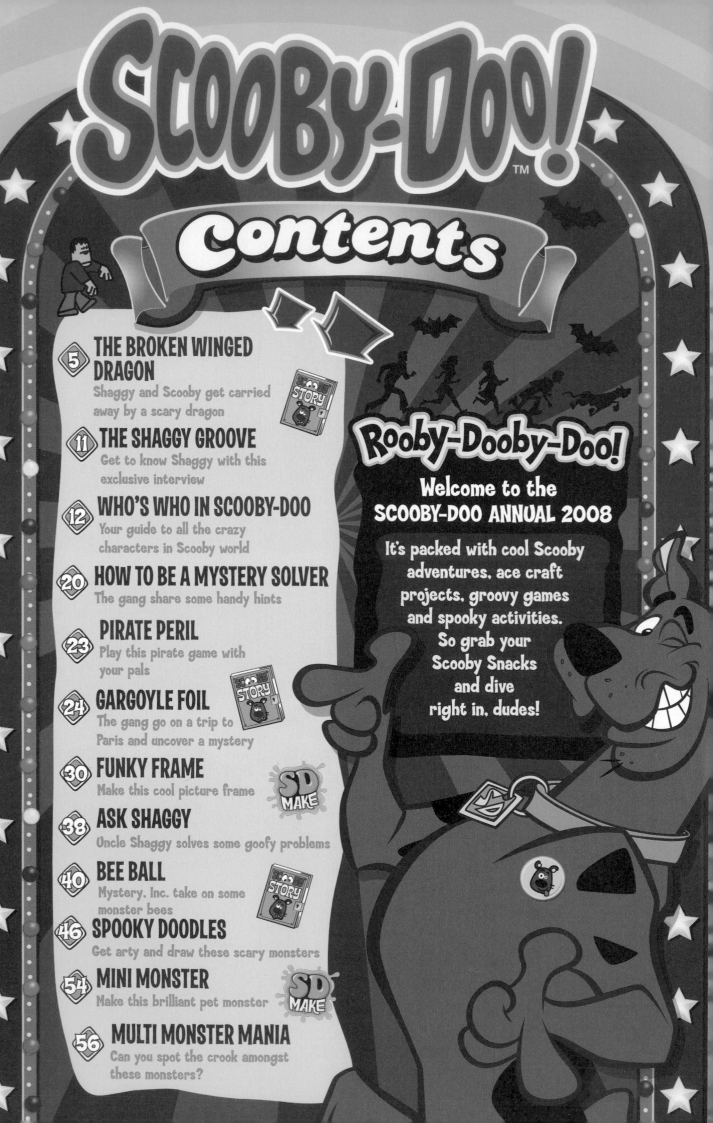

SCOOBY-DOO!

Contents

Rooby-Dooby-Doo!

Welcome to the
SCOOBY-DOO ANNUAL 2008

It's packed with cool Scooby adventures, ace craft projects, groovy games and spooky activities.
So grab your Scooby Snacks and dive right in, dudes!

RURIK TYLER - WRITER
JOE STATON - PENCILS
ANDREW PEPOY - INKS

PAUL BECTON - COLORS
SNO CONE - SEPS
JARED K FLETCHER - LETTERS
HARVEY RICHARDS - ASST EDITOR
JOAN HILTY - EDITOR

SCOOBY-DOO 78. January, 2004. Published monthly by DC Comics, 1700 Broadway, New York, NY 10019. POSTMASTER: Send address changes to SCOOBY-DOO, DC Comics Subscriptions, P.O. Box 0528, Baldwin, NY 11510. Annual subscription rate (12 issues) $27.00. Canadian subscribers must add $12.00 for postage and GST. GST # is R125921072. All foreign countries must add $12.00 for postage. U.S. funds only. Copyright © 2004 Hanna-Barbera. All Rights Reserved. SCOOBY-DOO and all related characters and elements depicted herein are trademarks of and © Hanna-Barbera. CARTOON NETWORK and logo are trademarks of Cartoon Network. The stories, characters and incidents mentioned in this magazine are entirely fictional. Printed on recyclable paper. DC Comics does not read or accept unsolicited submissions of ideas, stories or artwork. Printed in Canada.

DC Comics, a Warner Bros. Entertainment Company

• DAN DIDIO, VP-Editorial • PAUL LEVITZ, President & Publisher • GEORG BREWER, VP-Design & Retail Product Development •
• RICHARD BRUNING, Sr. VP-Creative Director • PATRICK CALDON, Senior VP-Finance & Operations • CHRIS CARAMALIS, VP-Finance • TERRI CUNNINGHAM, VP-Managing Editor •
• ALISON GILL, VP-Manufacturing • LILLIAN LASERSON, Sr. VP & General Counsel • JIM LEE, Editorial Director-Wildstorm •
• DAVID McKILLIPS, VP-Advertising Custom Publishing • JOHN NEE, VP-Business Development •
• CHERYL RUBIN, VP-Brand Management • BOB WAYNE, VP-Sales & Marketing •

REALLY? A DRAGON? OF COURSE WE'LL HELP. WE'LL BE RIGHT OVER.

WHAT'S UP?

SOMEBODY'S SPOTTED A DRAGON OUT IN HUNTINGTON WOODS!

LIKE, HEY, WAIT A SECOND! WE'VE GOT THE PERFECT GEAR FOR THIS CASE!

TA-DA!! TIN-CAN TUXEDOES!!!

REAH! RIN-RAN RUHREEDOS!

OH BROTHER! GET BACK IN THE VAN!

ISN'T THAT THE EVIDENCE FROM THAT OLD HAUNTED ARMOR CASE? TAKE IT OFF, SHAG. WE MIGHT NEED YOU FOR DECOY WORK!

TOO BAD THE ARMOR WASN'T REALLY HAUNTED. WE COULD HAVE USED THE *GHOST* FOR THE DECOY WORK!

SOON...

HELLO, DAPHNE, I'D LIKE TO INTRODUCE YOU TO LISA. SHE SHOT ACTUAL VIDEOTAPE OF THE CREATURE!

TAPE?

YOU KNOW, THE DRAGON FOOTAGE.

LIKE, IF THEY'VE TAPED THE DRAGON'S FEET, WHAT DO THEY NEED US FOR?

OW! DARN FLY.

HI LISA. WE'RE *MYSTERY INCORPORATED.*

MYSTERY INCORPORATED? WHAT CHANNEL ARE YOU ON?

WE'RE NOT ON *ANY* CHANNEL. WE'RE NOT ON TV AT ALL.

OH, A WEBCAM SHOW?

WEBCAM OR NOT, THIS STORY IS OURS!

GET OUT OF HERE! THE TAPE OF THE DRAGON IS OURS!

UHM, THE TAPE IS MINE, AND I HAVEN'T DECIDED TO SELL IT YET.

COULD WE SEE THE TAPE, LISA?

THERE'S THE DRAGON EATING FRUIT FROM HIGH UP IN THE TREE. YOU CAN SEE ITS BODY, BUT ITS HEAD IS HIDDEN BY LEAVES!

I THOUGHT I COULD SNEAK CLOSER WHILE THE DRAGON WASN'T LOOKING--BUT IT MUST HAVE HEARD ME, BECAUSE IT CHARGED AS SOON AS I APPROACHED!

OKAY, LET'S TAKE A LOOK AT THE SITE.

RANGER JONES, MEET MYSTERY INC. AT THE SIGHTING ZONE!

YES SIR.

HEY! HOW COME THEY GET TO GO?

WOW. SOME PEOPLE WILL DO ANYTHING FOR RATINGS!

HELLO, FOLKS, THIS IS THE SPOT WHERE THE DRAGON WAS FILMED.

WHAT DO YOU THINK? IS IT A FRAUD?

I DON'T KNOW. THIS "DRAGON" LEFT A LOT OF DAMAGE. YOU SEE BEARS IN THESE WOODS ONCE IN A WHILE, BUT NOTHING BIG ENOUGH TO DO THIS!

THIS IS THE SPOT. BUT...

WHAT'S WRONG, FREDDY?

WELL, THERE AREN'T ANY FRUIT TREES!

OH MY GOSH, YOU'RE RIGHT. WHY WOULD LISA SAY THERE WERE?

I DON'T KNOW, BUT *THIS* MIGHT BE A CLUE.

LIKE, A *SCRAP OF PAPER* WITH THE TOPS OF SOME LETTERS ON IT!

WONDER WHAT IT SAYS?

LIKE, "IN CASE OF DRAGON, RIP SIGN"?

HMM. THERE ARE SO MANY "TRAILS" OF BROKEN PLANTS, WE HAVE NO WAY OF KNOWING WHICH ONE TO FOLLOW!

WAIT A MINUTE! DID YOU SAY THAT PAPER MIGHT BE A CLUE? BECAUSE THERE'S SOME MORE OF IT ON THAT TRAIL OVER THERE!

THERE'S A CREEK IN THAT DIRECTION--MAYBE THE "DRAGON" WENT TO GET A DRINK.

YEAH, LIKE BREATHING FIRE MAKES YOU THIRSTY.

CONTINUED ON PAGE 14

The Coolsville Bugle

NOVEMBER 2007

EXCLUSIVE INTERVIEW!

The Shaggy Groove!

Groovy dude Shaggy Rogers

Hey there, Shaggy! How are you?

Like, I'm super-cool, thanks! We've just got back from solving a spooky mystery so I'm ready to kick back on my sofa and have a snooze!

Well done! Was it really spooky?

A screaming banshee was being a nuisance in a castle. Fred made a trap using a fishing net and a teapot and a cushion with Scooby as the bait. We managed to get that crazy lady all tied up!

Sounds totally spine-tingling! How are the rest of the Mystery, Inc. crew?

Like, they are all totally awesome! The Scoobster is busy cooking some Scooby Snacks at the moment.

What's the best thing about being a mystery solver?

Getting to hang out with my best buds. The worst thing is the monsters, I could totally do without them!

You recently won the Coolsville Waffle Eating Competition! Well done, you must be very proud!

Like, thanks, dude! That was one of the most tip-top days ever. I ate 25 banana and chocolate waffles in 1 minute 8 seconds, it was awesome!

Our readers love your groovy brown flares. Where do you buy them?

Like, my fab flares are just the best! My Uncle Norbert makes them for me. The best bit is, they have a pocket in the back designed for holding a spoon. Then I'm always prepared for a snack attack!

Have you got a cool secret you can share with our readers?

Hmm, lemme see. Fred is really brave but he gets totally spooked by centipedes! It's all those legs, they give him the shivers! Hee hee!

who's who in → SCOOBY-DOO! ™

Find out all there is to know about Scooby-Doo and his crazy mystery-packed world!

The Gang

The members of the Mystery, Inc. crew are Fred Jones, Daphne Blake, Shaggy Rogers, Velma Dinkley and Scooby-Doo.

Fred is the leader of the gang but each member plays an important part in solving mysteries.

The Mystery Machine

The Mystery Machine transports the gang to wherever their latest mystery is taking place. With a top speed of 60 mph, it may not be very fast but its nimble steering means it can be relied upon to catch any hot-footed crook.

The van was decorated by Scooby-Doo and Shaggy, check out those groovy flowers! In the back of th van you will find Daphne photography dark room, a mini kitchen, a rope lasso and a monster net.

Scooby Snacks

These tasty little biscuits are a Scooby-Doo essential and no mystery would get solved without them. They are Scooby and Shaggy's favourite snack and they come in very handy for bribing the scaredy pair into tackling monsters.

It's a Ghost Town

Mystery, Inc. live in a spook-packed town called Coolsville. Their favourite spot to hang out is The Malt Shop, a funky café on the Coolsville Main Street.

The town is packed with haunted museums, castles, graveyards and libraries. In fact, a mystery lurks behind every corner in this ghost town!

THE VILLIANS!

Redbeard the Pirate

Redbeard is the captain of a ghost ship. He and his ghostly crew emerge from the fog and steal from other boats.

Spooky-Doo!

Mystery, Inc. have taken on all shapes and sizes of supernatural baddies. Check out some of their arch enemies.

The Witch Doctor

The gang first encountered the Witch Doctor when they were on holiday in Hawaii. This creepy character is a master of black magic and is a tough villain to take on.

Alien Encounters

Monsters from outer space are something the gang are very familiar with. Whether it's mysterious lights in the sky or angry aliens on the rampage, the gang never gets spooked by martian meddlers.

The Zombie

The gang have tackled a variety of zombies, or the Living Dead, as they are also known. This particular green meanie loves to wander around graveyards and make people jump.

The Mummy

While the gang were exploring the Forbidden Pyramid in Egypt, they unleashed a terrifying 2000-year-old mummy. Poor Scooby was terrified of that wrapped-up baddy!

RATCH ROUT, RAGGY!

SCOOB!

ZOINKS! HERE IT COMES, OLD BUDDY!

RAGGY!

IT'S A BUNCH OF KIDS!

STAY IN THE FRAME! STAY IN THE FRAME!

HEY! WATCH YOUR FEET! LOOK OUT!

OH MY ANKLE!

LOOKS LIKE YOU SPRAINED IT. HOLD STILL.

SO THE WHOLE THING WAS A FAKE AFTER ALL?

WHAT FAKE? WE JUST NEEDED DRAGON FOOTAGE.

VELMA?

YES, SHAGGY?

IF THE DRAGON'S FEET ARE FAKE, WHAT DO THEY NEED US FOR?

SO WHAT'S WITH THE FAKE DRAGON COSTUME?

THE NEWSLADY SAID SHE'D PAY US IF WE HELPED HER GET SOME DRAGON FOOTAGE. WE WANTED TO GET IN ON THE ACTION!

IF THEY WERE TRYING TO GET "IN" ON THE ACTION, IT MEANS THAT THEY WERE NOT THE ORIGINAL DRAGON.

UHM, GUYS, WHY IS THE GROUND SHAKING?

MAYBE IT'S *ANOTHER* GROUP OF KIDS.

MAYBE IT'S...

...THE *DRAGON!!!*

WHY IS HE COMING AFTER ME? DID THIS HELMET BELONG TO SOMEONE HE USED TO KNOW? *HERE!* HAVE IT BACK!

RUN, SHAGGY, *RUN!* DAPHNE, GET *THAT CLUE!*

OKAY, BUT WE'VE GOT TO HELP SHAGGY!

AAAH! THIS THING NEEDS SEATBELTS!

ARE YOU GUYS ALL RIGHT?

RELLLLMA?

I DON'T KNOW WHAT THAT WAS, BUT I KNOW WE HAVE TO GET THIS ANKLE TREATED. YOU KIDS BETTER COME TOO!

DAPHNE, CAN YOU SEE ANYTHING WHEN YOU PUT THE SCRAPS TOGETHER?

THIS LETTERING IS VERY ORNATE. CAN YOU MAKE OUT WHAT IT SAYS?

IT LOOKS LIKE IT SAYS "FAR"...NO. WAIT!

DO YOU SEE THE DOT OF THE *I*? IT SAYS *FAIR!* OOH! RANGER JONES, MAY I BORROW YOUR RADIO?

HELLO, CHIEF? ARE ANY FAIRS SCHEDULED FOR THE AREA?

LET ME CHECK MY NOTEBOOK.--HEY NOW! LOOK AT THAT! VELMA, YOU JUST CRACKED THE CASE!

THE CHIEF SAYS YOU CRACKED THE CASE--SO TELL US-- WHAT'S GOING ON?

BEATS ME!

WELL, PUT IT OUT OF YOUR MIND FOR THE NEXT HOUR OR SO UNTIL WE GET OUT, AND LET'S TRY TO GET AS FAR FROM THE "DRAGON" AS POSSIBLE.

LIKE, DO YOU THINK WE CAN GET AWAY FROM THE DRAGON?

WELL, SO FAR IT HASN'T COME INTO THIS SECTION OF THE WOODS --SO MAYBE.

BOY, I HOPE YOU'RE RIGHT!

JUST KEEP MOVING. WE'RE ALMOST OUT NOW!

RE RAR? RATS RATE!

WHAT'S THAT?! THERE IN THE SKY!?

IT'S THE DRAGON! IT'S FLYING!

I DON'T BELIEVE IT!

IT'S A *HOT AIR BALLOON!*

EVERYONE, THIS IS *MONSIEUR PHILLIPE* OF *MONSIEUR PHILLIPE'S ROYAL RENAISSANCE FAIR.* THE "DRAGON" BELONGS TO HIM!

THE DRAGON IS ACTUALLY A *TRAINED ELEPHANT* IN AN *ELABORATE COSTUME.* HE GOT SEPARATED FROM THE FAIR, AND OO-LA-LA, HE GETS CRANKY IF HE IS IN COSTUME FOR MORE THAN A HALF HOUR!

NOW IT ALL MAKES SENSE! THE *FURROWS* AND *MUD SPATTERS* WERE THE ELEPHANT TRYING TO COAT ITS SKIN TO KEEP THOSE *BITING FLIES* AWAY.

AND THE REASON IT WAS *EATING* IN A TREE WITHOUT ANY FRUIT IS THAT IT WAS *EATING* THE *LEAVES.*

SO, THE REASON IT COULD SEE THE COUNSELOR *SNEAKING* UP ON IT WITH ITS *HEAD* IN THE LEAVES WAS THAT THAT WAS ITS *TRUNK!* THE ELEPHANT WAS LOOKING AT HER THE *WHOLE* TIME.

WOW! IT REALLY WAS AN ELEPHANT IN A COSTUME! WE FACED A LOOSE, CHARGING ELEPHANT!

WHAT'S THE *BIG* DEAL? ELEPHANTS AREN'T EVEN SUPERNATURAL --SO WHAT?

WELL, GET HIM--YOU'D THINK HE'D LIVED ALL HIS LIFE NEXT TO AN ELEPHANT GRAVEYARD OR SOMETHING!

GR-GRAVE-YARD? I'M GOING TO FAINT--OOOO..

UH-OH. WE'D BETTER MAKE SOME MORE ROOM ON THAT STRETCHER.

HA HA HA HA HA

THE END

HOW TO BE A MYSTERY SOLVER!

So you reckon you've got what it takes to mash monsters?

Then you'll need Mystery, Inc's handy dandy guide on how to be a mystery solver!

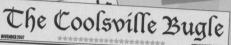

STEP 1: Find a Mystery

The first task is to find yourself a mystery to solve. This is what you need to do to find yourself a ghoul-packed mystery.

The Coolsville Bugle
NOVEMBER 2007 — ONLY 3 SCOOBY SNACKS!

Blood Thirsty Dracula On the Loose

NEW CLUES FOUND! Pages 2, 3 and 4

There are spooky mysteries lurking everywhere, you just have to know where to look!

Keep your eyes peeled and check out the local newspaper. The Coolsville Bugle is a great place to start as it is always full of stories about vampires and mud monsters causing trouble.

According to Velma, a spooky stanger rolling into town can often lead to a mystery. Watch out for kooky people with any of the following:

1. HAIRY HANDS AND LONG TALONS

2. A HAT (IT'S PROBAB HIDING THEIR ANTENNA AND MONSTER EARS.)

3. EYES THAT GLOW IN THE DARK

STEP 2: Clue Spotting

Fred always says that a mystery never gets solved until those clues get found! This is how to spot them...

DRY ICE MACHINE
ON OFF

Velma says: Spoof spooks use creepy mist to disguise what they are really up to. Look out for a dry ice machine and you'll know it's fake fog.

Daphne says: Even if a ghost appears to be floating there is always a logical explanation. Check the area where the ghost appeared. Footprints on the ground are a giveaway that it's simply a bad guy up to no good!

Shaggy says: Like, keep your peepers peeled and look out for pots of phosphorescent paint. Baddies use it to make them glow in a spooky way!

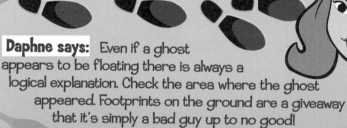

WOOO!

WOOO!

STEP 3: Escape Routes

Sometimes chasing a monster can go wrong and you end up with them chasing you! Here are some tips for when the chase is on.

Run, run, run!

Run as fast as you can with your hair on end and your mouth wide open as you shout "Heeeeeeeelp!"

Super Skates

Speed up your escape with a handy pair of roller skates. No monster can out-run a skating Scooby!

Bookcase bonus

Stop to press a few books in the bookcase, it's bound to reveal a hidden escape route!

Dress it up

Always carry a fancy dress costume which you can pull on in an emergency. That silly monster will never suspect an old lady or a tree of actually being you!

STEP 4: Set a Trap

Once you have got that monster cornered, you need to get it tied up in a trap. Fred shares his handy hints for trap building...

1 Take some time to design your trap and remember, make it as elaborate as you can. That way, the monster will never suspect it's a trap!

2 The bait for your trap is vital because it will lead the monster into the centre of the trap. Scooby-Doo and Shaggy work perfectly!

3 Once that monster is tied up, it's your job to swoop in and remove the monster's mask. This is the best bit of the job so don't be afraid to shout "Ta-daa!" each time!

21

Roll up, roll up!

Use your detective skills to spot all of the words hidden in the grid below.

S	T	U	N	O	C	O	C	M	B	A	F
G	H	O	S	T	T	R	A	I	N	P	E
I	S	E	T	B	G	C	O	R	I	P	R
S	T	H	O	T	D	O	G	R	O	N	R
S	E	D	I	R	G	R	Y	O	R	O	I
O	A	V	E	B	R	A	S	R	A	B	S
L	C	R	B	R	E	K	M	S	O	E	W
F	L	A	E	A	Z	E	E	E	R	K	H
Y	T	L	E	L	T	O	G	A	S	A	E
D	L	P	N	K	L	H	D	E	R	Y	E
N	R	O	A	C	A	R	O	U	S	E	L
A	T	O	C	S	W	L	D	C	R	A	V
C	I	H	S	I	F	D	L	O	G	V	

HOT DOG
FERRIS WHEEL
DODGEMS
GHOST TRAIN
CAROUSEL

GAMES
CANDY FLOSS
SIDESHOW
MIRRORS
WALTZER

COCONUTS
GOLDFISH
RIDES
HOOPLA

There is one word which doesn't appear in the grid. Can you work out which one it is?

Answer: sideshow

22

PIRATE PERIL!

Ahoy there, m'hearties! Play this pirate game with your friends and see who is the first shipmate to make it to the crow's nest.

24

25 REDBEARD THE GHOST MAKES YOU JUMP! HIDE BEHIND SPACE 23

26

27

28

29 YOU'RE THE WINNER!

23

22

21 WALK THE PLANK! GO BACK TO SPACE 15

20

19

18 YOU FIND SOME PIRATE TREASURE. TAKE ANOTHER TURN

12

13

14

15

16 WALK THE PLANK! GO BACK TO SPACE 8

17

11

10

9 WALK THE PLANK! GO BACK TO SPACE 1

8

7

6 SHIVER M'TIMBERS! TAKE ANOTHER TURN

START

1

2

3 STOP TO CHAT TO THE CAPTAIN'S PARROT. MISS A TURN

4

5

PIECES OF EIGHT

How to play:

Play the game with a friend. Take it in turns to throw a dice and move around the game board. The first player to reach the crow's nest is the winner, just be careful you don't walk the plank and land in shark-infested water!

SCOOBY STORY

GARGOYLE FOIL

I QUIT!

WHY?

A BETTER QUESTION, SISTER MARIE, WOULD BE *WHY* WE MUST SPEAK *HERE*, IN THE NORTH TOWER OF THE CATHEDRAL, WITH ITS *BELLS* AND ITS *BATS?* I *HATE* BELLS! I *HATE* BATS!

AS FOR YOUR "WHY"--I RESIGN BECAUSE THE CATHEDRAL IS *HAUNTED!*

TERRENCE GRIEP, JR.-WRITER
KAREN MATCHETTE-PENCILLER
SCOTT MCRAE-INKER
NICK J. NAP-LETTERER • HEROIC AGE-COLORIST
HARVEY RICHARDS-ASST. EDITOR • JOAN HILTY-EDITOR

THAT'S IT, GANG. ONE OF THE MOST FAMOUS CATHEDRALS IN THE WORLD--THE *CATHEDRAL OF NOTRE DAME!*

IT'S SUCH A THRILL TO BE IN *PARIS!*

THE GARGOYLES HAVE *FAILED,* SISTER MARIE!

G-GUH-GARGOYLES? *WHERE?*

THE STONE GARGOYLES OF THE CATHEDRAL ARE MEANT TO PROTECT IT FROM EVIL SPIRITS, BUT THEY HAVE FAILED THEIR DUTY! HENCE, THE *GHOST!* HENCE, I QUIT! AND SO--*ADIEU!*

THE WORD "GARGOYLE" IS DERIVED FROM LATIN FOR "GULLET" OR "DRAIN," SHAGGY. YOU DON'T FIND DRAINS SCARY, DO YOU?

W-WUH-WELL...

I AM SO SORRY THAT THIS *PROBLEM* IS INTERRUPTING YOUR TOUR OF NOTRE DAME DE PARIS...

THAT'S ALL RIGHT, SISTER MARIE. WE'RE ACTUALLY QUITE USED TO THIS SORT OF THING. WHAT'S THIS ABOUT THE CATHEDRAL BEING HAUNTED?

OH, IT IS NOTHING. JUST THE ANGRY RAVINGS OF OUR GARDENER...OUR *FORMER* GARDENER, JACQUES LAURENT. HE IS MERELY A--HOW DO YOU AMERICANS PUT IT?--AH, A *DISGRUNTLED EMPLOYEE.*

DON'T BE SO SURE, SISTER--!

LIKE, WHO'RE YOU?

WHO AM I? WHY, I AM RENE-OLANAIS, THE DIRECTOR OF THE *CATHEDRAL CHOIR.* I CAME UP HERE TO DEMAND *QUIET* --YOU MAKE MORE *NOISE* THAN THE BELLS THEMSELVES!

ACTUALLY, RENE, THE BELLS ARE *SILENT*. THE CATHEDRAL IS BEING RENOVATED. THUS, THE UNSIGHTLY SCAFFOLDING AND ROPES...

ZUT! TOURISTS! *ALWAYS* THE TOURISTS! MY JOB WOULD BE SO MUCH MORE GRATIFYING IF NOT FOR *YOU* TOURISTS!

AND THEN I HEAR SISTER MARIE SAYING THAT THE CATHEDRAL IS NOT HAUNTED. *PHAH--!* OVER THE PAST FEW WEEKS, THINGS HAVE BEEN *DISAPPEARING!*

THINGS?

A SONG BOOK HERE, A CROISSANT THERE--OUR GHOST, HE THINKS *SMALL!*

LIKE, THE THEFT OF *FOOD* IS NEVER "SMALL," MONSIEUR!

REAH!

WELL, THERE COULD BE A LOT OF REASONS FOR THOSE DISAPPEARANCES. THAT DOESN'T MEAN THE CATHEDRAL IS *HAUNTED.*

PERHAPS NOT...

...BUT PERHAPS *THIS* DOES! SISTER, I BRING DIRE NEWS!

JEAN CORSAIR? IS THERE A PROBLEM IN THE *OFFICE?*

MY DUTIES AS THE CATHEDRAL'S UNDERPAID *SECRETARY* DO NOT BRING ME HERE, ALAS. I AM HERE TO INFORM YOU THAT THE *GOLDEN MAIDEN* IS MISSING!

OH, BOY. WHO ELSE BUT MYSTERY, INC. COULD TURN A NIFTY TOUR OF PARIS INTO A *CRIME SCENE?* I MEAN, THIS CATHEDRAL IS ONE LOVELY LADY, Y'DIG?

RADY?

YEAH, SCOOB. "NOTRE DAME" MEANS "OUR LADY," WHICH REFERS TO SAINT MARY.

AND, LIKE, WHY WOULD A GHOST COME HERE, TO *CITE ISLAND* ON THE *SEINE RIVER?*

WHY, SHAGGY-- I'M *IMPRESSED!* HOW DO YOU KNOW SO MUCH ABOUT THE CATHEDRAL?

LIKE, I JUST LEARNED IT FROM THE *POSTCARDS* IN THE *GIFT SHOP!*

THE *GOLDEN MAIDEN!* SHE IS ONE OF THE CATHEDRAL'S MOST *PRIZED EFFECTS!* THIS CANNOT BE!

RHE ROLDEN RAIDEN?

YEAH. I'VE GOT A POSTCARD OF IT RIGHT HERE! IT'S A STATUE OF SAINT MARY, MADE OF *PURE GOLD!*

WELL, GANG, LOOKS LIKE WE'VE GOT ANOTHER *MYSTERY* ON OUR HANDS. SISTER MARIE, IF IT'S OKAY WITH YOU, WE'D LIKE TO HELP YOU GET THE GOLDEN MAIDEN BACK!

I HAVE FAITH THAT YOU WILL, CHILDREN. WE SHALL CLOSE THE PONT-NEUF BRIDGE THAT CONNECTS US TO THE REST OF PARIS! CITE ISLAND IS HEREBY *QUARANTINED!*

CONTINUED ON PAGE 32

Funky Frame!

This brilliant Mystery Machine frame is a great way to display your favourite photos

YOU WILL NEED:

Thick card,
scissors,
a ruler,
PVA glue,
newspaper,
paints and a
paintbrush,
a plastic lid.

HANDY HINT!

Attach some string to the back of the frame if you want to hang it on the wall. Or you can tape a triangle of card on the back so that it can stand on a shelf.

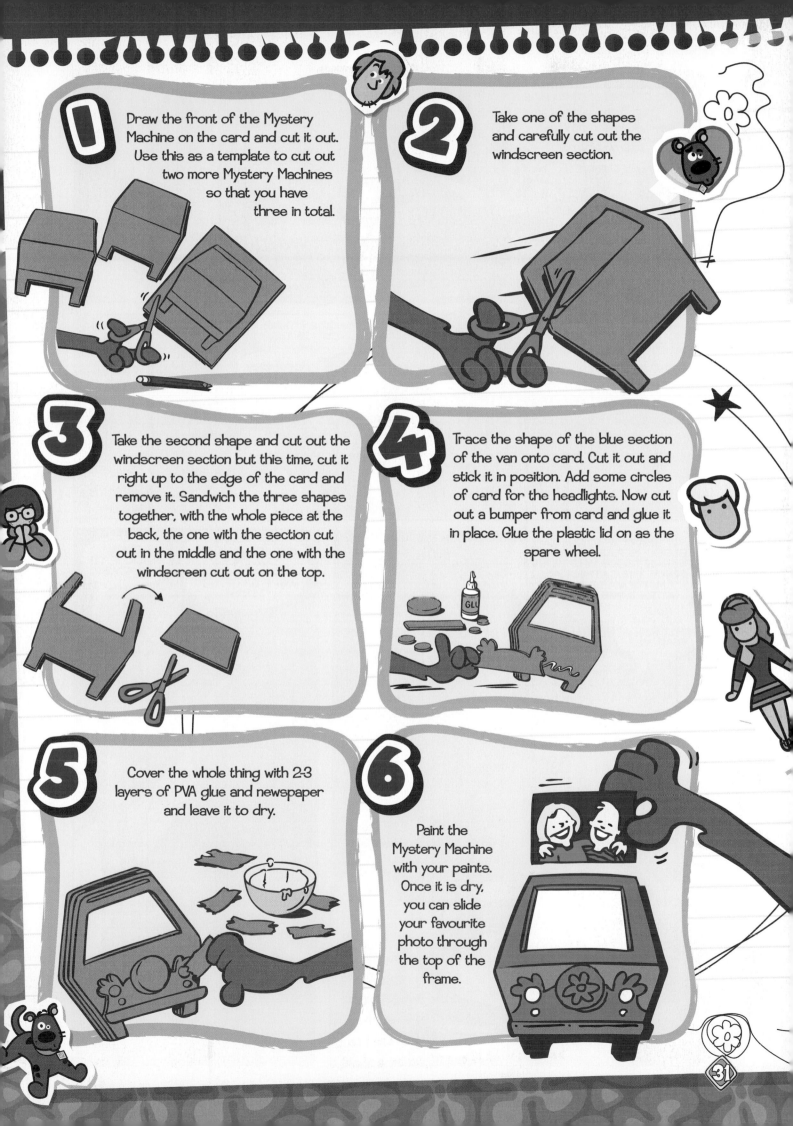

1 Draw the front of the Mystery Machine on the card and cut it out. Use this as a template to cut out two more Mystery Machines so that you have three in total.

2 Take one of the shapes and carefully cut out the windscreen section.

3 Take the second shape and cut out the windscreen section but this time, cut it right up to the edge of the card and remove it. Sandwich the three shapes together, with the whole piece at the back, the one with the section cut out in the middle and the one with the windscreen cut out on the top.

4 Trace the shape of the blue section of the van onto card. Cut it out and stick it in position. Add some circles of card for the headlights. Now cut out a bumper from card and glue it in place. Glue the plastic lid on as the spare wheel.

5 Cover the whole thing with 2-3 layers of PVA glue and newspaper and leave it to dry.

6 Paint the Mystery Machine with your paints. Once it is dry, you can slide your favourite photo through the top of the frame.

...SO DAPHNE, SISTER MARIE, AND I WILL SEARCH THE *WEST FACADE*, WHILE SHAGGY, SCOOBY, AND VELMA WILL SEARCH THE *SOUTH PORTAL*.

AND FOR WHAT ARE WE SEARCHING?

FOR ANYTHING OUT OF THE, UH...

...ORDINARY?

MY HEART IS STONE...MY BLOOD IS RAIN! I INSPIRE FEAR IN THOSE WHO WOULD HARM THE CATHEDRAL! I AM THE GARGOYLE OF NOTRE DAME DE PARIS!

FEAR ME, YOU CHILDREN-- FEAR ME!

HEAVEN HELP US! A GARGOYLE COME TO LIFE!

HEY, FRED-- IF I SEE ANYTHING OUT OF THE ORDINARY, I'LL BE SURE TO LET YOU KNOW!

QUICK! BACK UP TO THE TOWER!

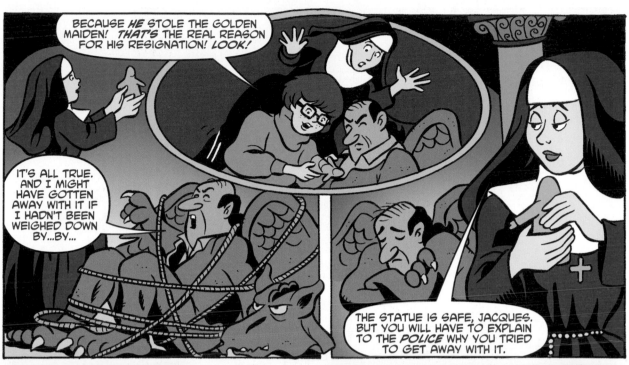

BECAUSE *HE* STOLE THE GOLDEN MAIDEN! *THAT'S* THE REAL REASON FOR HIS RESIGNATION! *LOOK!*

IT'S ALL TRUE. AND I MIGHT HAVE GOTTEN AWAY WITH IT IF I HADN'T BEEN WEIGHED DOWN BY...BY...

THE STATUE IS SAFE, JACQUES. BUT YOU WILL HAVE TO EXPLAIN TO THE *POLICE* WHY YOU TRIED TO GET AWAY WITH IT.

BUT WHAT ABOUT THE *SMALLER* THEFTS? THEY WERE JUST OUR NEW FRIEND TAKING WHAT HE NEEDED TO LIVE.

HE'S JUST BEEN AFRAID OF PEOPLE UP UNTIL NOW. PLEASE, SISTER MARIE--DON'T PUNISH HIM!

REAL FAITH IS BASED ON FORGIVENESS, NOT PUNISHMENT. BUT THE POSITION OF *GARDENER* IS OPEN--THAT IS, IF YOUR...IF *OUR* FRIEND IS INTERESTED!

HEH. LIKE, I THINK THAT'S A *YES*--OR A "OUI"!

HA HA HA HA HA HA HA HA

END

Dear Shaggy

Dear Shaggy,

Help! There's a gremlin living in my understairs cupboard and I don't know what to do! He is small, green and has bad breath. What should I do to get rid of him?

Your desperately,
Ivor Monster

Zoinks! Like, my advice to you is to move house! If that isn't totally practical, maybe you could push a note under the cupboard door saying "Dear Mr. Gremlin, please will you go away? Like, thanks!". If that doesn't work, give Freddie a shout, he'll scare it away for ya!

horrible, stinkin' little gremlin

Dear Shaggy,

Can you help my friend and I to settle an argument? I reckon a werewolf is the scariest monster to tackle, but she says vampires are worse because they are scary and clever. Which one is the scariest monster?

Your gratefully,
Elma Spookafinkle

Like, I gotta tell you, they both give me the heebie jeebies! Although vampires never come near me cos I'm always eating garlic pizza with chilli-garlic sauce. That's the way to keep those bad guys away!

Dracula **VS.** Werewolf

CHILLI

Dear Shaggy,

My pet pooch sleeps on my sofa and he snores really loudly. Plus he is a big hairy mongrel and there is never any room for me to sit on the sofa. What should I do?

Thanks, Mr Hound

Now this is one problemo that I can totally relate to, dude! The Scoobster never lets me near the sofa! One trick is to put out a bowl of Scooby Snacks and then jump on the sofa when he isn't looking. As for the snoring, just be glad he doesn't howl in his sleep like Scooby, now that really is noisy!

Zzzz

Zzzz

FUN AT THE FAIR!

Daphne and Velma have discovered some spooky shadows in the fairground. Can you work out what each shadow belongs to?

B A C 1 2 D 4 3 E 6 5 G 7 I H 9 F 8

A B C D E F G H I

AURIK TYLER • writer JOE STATON • pencils
DAVE HUNT • inks JOHN COSTANZA • letters
PAUL BECTON • colors HARVEY RICHARDS • asst editor
JOAN HILTY • editor

CONTINUED ON PAGE 48

45

SPOOKY DOODLES!

Have a go at drawing your own scary scene, filled with monsters and ghosts.

Goony Ghost

Grab a pencil and follow the steps below to draw your own cartoon ghost.

Start by drawing a circle with an oval shape on top. Add lines for the mouth and circles for the eyes. Sketch in the arms and hands and add a wiggly cone shape on the top of the head. Finally, add the details and once you are happy with the shape, draw over it in pen.

BOO!

Oh Mummy!

Now try drawing a mad mummy!

The sketch starts with a triangle for the main part of the body and smaller triangles for the arms and legs. Add circles for hands, feet and eyes. Now sketch in lots of thin lines for the bandages. Don't forget to add some tatty pieces of bandage to make him look manky!

RIP

Awesome Alien

This cute alien is out of this world!

1. Start by drawing a long sausage shape.
2. Add a flat base and a circle at the top.
3. Sketch in two long thin wiggly arms, two small triangles for antennae and a smiley mouth.
4. Add the hands, feet and spots. Give the monster a wobbly outline and colour the sketch in with your favourite colours.

1

2

3

4

et Doodling!

Poor Scooby-Doo is looking totally spooked! Have a go at adding some monsters to the scene.

HEY! THEY SPLIT UP!

I SAY WE FOLLOW THE BEES!

THAT'S WHAT I THINK TOO!

YIKES! WHAT HAPPENED? THIS PLACE SURE TURNED GLOOMY FAST.

THIS IS A CASE OF A LAND DEAL LOOKING FOR A GHOST.

WEIRD, LOOK AT ALL THE SPORTS EQUIPMENT. BUT NO SIGN OF THE BEES!

LET'S HAVE A LOOK AROUND.

EVERYTHING IS ADVANCING AS WE HAD HOPED!

YES, AND TONIGHT WE BEGIN PLAN "B"-- HEH, HEH, HEH... I LOVE SAYING THAT!

YEAH, WAIT UNTIL THE TOWNSPEOPLE GET A LOAD OF US... HEY, WHAT WAS THAT NOISE?

INTRUDERS! GET 'EM!

UH OH!

MINI MONSTER!

Zoinks! Have you seen that scary monster? Follow the steps to create your own monster pet.

Arrrgh!

YOU WILL NEED:

Newspaper, a balloon, two long cardboard tubes, PVA glue, kitchen paper, sticky tape, scissors, paints and a paintbrush.

1 Blow up a balloon and cover it with 3-4 layers of torn-up newspaper and glue. Leave it to dry

2 Cut one of the cardboard tubes into four pieces and cut the other tube in half.

Scrunch up six balls of newspaper and tape one to the end of each cardboard tube. Cover with newspaper and glue and leave to dry.

3 Pop the balloon. Use lots of sticky tape to attach the two longer cardboard tubes to the pointed end of the balloon. These will be his eye stalks.

4 Use sticky tape to attach the four shorter tubes to the rounded end of the balloon. These will make his legs.

5 Use rolled-up sausages of kitchen paper to mould his eyelids, mouth and nostrils.

Finally, when your monster is dry, you can paint him! Try some polka dots, crazy stripes or multi-coloured splats to create a really hairy-scary monster!

Rikes!

MULTI-MONSTER MANIA!

JOHN ROZUM- WRITER
JOE STATON- PENCILLER
SCOTT MCRAE- INKER

JARED FLETCHER- LETTERER
HEROIC AGE- COLORIST
HARVEY RICHARDS- ASST. EDITOR
JOAN HILTY- EDITOR

ACCORDING TO THOSE WITNESSES WHO SAW THE NECKLACE THEFT, THE MONSTER CAME THIS WAY.

THEN SHOULDN'T WE BE GOING THE *OTHER* WAY?

SCOOBY STORY

I WISH WE'D HAD A CHANCE TO *SEE* IT OURSELVES.

NONE OF THOSE WITNESSES COULD *AGREE* ON WHAT IT LOOKED LIKE.

THE ONLY THING THEY DID AGREE ON WAS THAT IT WAS *SHAGGY.*

RAGGY?!

ME?!

"SHAGGY" AS IN "HAIRY..."

...OR IN THIS CASE, *FURRY.*

ARE YOU SURE THAT'S FROM OUR MONSTER AND NOT SOME ANIMAL?

NOT UNLESS YOU CAN NAME AN ANIMAL WITH *GREEN* FUR....

IT'S OUR *FIRST* CLUE!

...HERE.

OH NO, IT'S A COSTUME PARTY! WE DON'T KNOW *WHICH* MONSTER IS OURS!

THAT DOESN'T MATTER. THERE ARE ONLY *SIX* MONSTERS IN THIS ROOM. LET'S LINE 'EM UP...

USING THE *CLUES* WE HAVE, WE CAN FIGURE OUT *WHICH* ONE IS THE MONSTER WE'RE AFTER!

???

NOW, *USING* THE *CLUES* FOUND ON THE BEACH, CAN YOU FIND WHICH MONSTER MYSTERY, INC. IS LOOKING FOR?

HERE'S OUR MONSTER!

LIKE, HOW DID YOU KNOW?

REAH, HROW?

SIMPLE. THE FUR I FOUND ON THE HURRICANE FENCE WAS *GREEN*, WHICH RULED OUT *TWO* OF THE MONSTERS RIGHT AWAY.

ALSO, THE FOOTPRINTS WE DISCOVERED HAD *THREE TOES*. THAT ELIMINATED ANOTHER OF THE MONSTERS AS A POSSIBILITY.

FINALLY, OUR MONSTER HAD *TWO CURVING HORNS* UPON ITS HEAD, WHICH ELIMINATED THE OTHER *TWO* SUSPECTS.

NOW TO SEE WHO HE *REALLY* IS...

IT'S *MONTY O'BURR*, THE PASTRY CHEF!

AND THERE'S THE STOLEN NECKLACE!

IT WOULD STILL BE MINE-- IF IT WEREN'T FOR YOU *MEDDLING MONSTER HUNTERS!*

ROOBY ROOBY ROO!

THE END

Wish you were here!

The gang have gone on a camping holiday but not everything is what it seems. Use your detective skills to spot all the characters hidden in the scene.

The marshmallows and hot dogs will have to wait until the fearless crew get to the bottom of this hair-raising mystery. Study the scene and see if you can spot all the gang. Then take another look and find these other crazy characters.

Treasure map

Timber Buck

The Werewolf

Ranger Rickity

Scooby-Doo-BBQ

Forest Stump

CRAZY MAZE TRAIL

BEAR GUIDE

CAMP POISON IVY

PUP TENT

SNAKE LAKE

SCREAMING STREAM

HALL OF MIRRORS!